The
HAM
HOUSE
KITCHEN

The larder DRESSER BOARDS and SHELVES were copied from this picture, as was the kitchen FORM. Note how the food is stored on PEWTER PLATES.

Wenceslaus Hollar, *Aesop's Fables*, London, 1665.

# The
# HAM
# HOUSE
## KITCHEN
*by*
# CAROLINE DAVIDSON

HAM HOUSE *is a property of the* NATIONAL TRUST
*administered by the* VICTORIA *and* ALBERT MUSEUM

*Published by the*
VICTORIA *and* ALBERT MUSEUM
ISBN 0 905209 93 1

*Copyright*
Caroline Davidson

*Designed by*
Grundy & Northedge Designers

*Printed by*
Royle Print Ltd., London

◆ ◆ ◆

*Photographs of the kitchen*
Sir Geoffrey Shakerley

*Front cover:*
The kitchen, showing the fire with its
mechanical spit-jack.

*Back cover:*
The larder

# HAM HOUSE
## *near Richmond, Surrey*

HAM HOUSE is a property of the National Trust, administered by the Victoria and Albert Museum.

Originally built in 1610 by Sir Thomas Vavasour as a modest country residence, Ham House was enlarged and modernised by the Duke and Duchess of Lauderdale in the 1670s and contains most of the paintings and furniture from the period.

It is open all year, Tuesday to Sunday inclusive, 11.00 to 17.00.
Closed Good Friday, May Day Bank Holiday, Christmas Eve, Christmas Day, Boxing Day and New Year's Day. Open on other Bank Holidays.

Guided tours can be arranged through the Education Department, Victoria and Albert Museum, South Kensington, London SW7 2RL. Telephone: 01-589 6371, ext. 316 or 258.

Other houses *administered by the*
# VICTORIA *and* ALBERT MUSEUM

◆ ◆ ◆

## APSLEY HOUSE
## THE WELLINGTON MUSEUM
*149 Piccadilly, London W1*

APSLEY HOUSE, sometimes called 'Number One, London' was the home of the first Duke of Wellington, famous for his success in the Peninsula War, and later a leading statesman. He acquired the house from his brother Marquis Wellesley in 1817 and in the late 1820s employed Benjamin Dean Wyatt to create the present house, which encases the original brick house built by Robert Adam in the 1770s. The Duke's magnificent picture gallery contains paintings from the Spanish royal collection and among the many masterpieces displayed at the house are the Portuguese centrepiece and the Waterloo shield which commemorates his success at the Battle of Waterloo, 1815.

Open all year, Tuesday, Wednesday, Thursday and Saturday: 10.00 to 18.00. Sunday: 14.30 to 18.00.
Closed Good Friday, May Day Bank Holiday, Christmas Eve, Christmas Day, Boxing Day and New Year's Day.

There are regular guided tours, usually on Thursday at 13.00. Details of these and other talks can be obtained from the programmes issued by the Education Department, Victoria and Albert Museum, South Kensington, London SW7 2RL. Telephone: 01-589 6371, ext. 316 or 258.
Groups can obtain the services of a qualified guide lecturer through the Education Department, Victoria and Albert Museum as above.

◆ ◆ ◆

## OSTERLEY PARK HOUSE
*Osterley, Middlesex*

OSTERLEY PARK HOUSE is a property of the National Trust, administered by the Victoria and Albert Museum.

An Elizabethan mansion transformed into an eighteenth-century villa with elegant neo-classical interior decoration designed by Robert Adam for the banker Robert Child. Osterley is remarkable in that it still boasts much of its eighteenth century decor and retains its grand Georgian furnishings. The antechamber of the state apartments is one of the few rooms in the world to remain in its entirety as it was in the 1770s.

Open all year, Tuesday to Sunday inclusive, 11.00 to 17.00.
Closed Good Friday, May Day Bank Holiday, Christmas Eve, Christmas Day, Boxing Day and New Year's Day. Open on other Bank Holidays.

Guided tours can be arranged through the Education Section, Victoria and Albert Museum, South Kensington, London SW7 2RL. Telephone: 589 6371; ext. 247 or 258.

◆ ◆ ◆

# The ORGANIZATION *of* domestic life *at* HAM HOUSE *during the* 1670s *and* early 1680s.

There were 15 'domestic offices' at Ham during the 1670s, all but one of them 'below stairs' in the basement:

The KITCHEN – where foods were boiled, stewed and spit roasted

The BAKE-HOUSE – where all the bread, cakes, biscuits and pies were baked in two brick ovens with iron doors

The DAIRY – where cream, butter and cheese were made

The STILL-HOUSE – where medicines, syrupy drinks, preserves and sweetmeats were concocted. It contained distilling equipment, chafing dishes, metal stoves for drying sweetmeats and an oven.

Two LARDERS – for weighing food; salting and preserving meat; storing provisions such as flour, eggs, vinegar, beef and bacon in tubs, barrels and casks; and keeping cooked 'leftovers' for the next meal

The SCULLERY – where birds were plucked, vegetables scrubbed and pewter washed

Four CELLARS – for storing beer and wine and plate (i.e. silver), as well as odds and ends like candles, dirty linen, eight plaster heads and a bathing tub

The USHER OF THE HALL'S OFFICE – his personal storeroom

The SERVANTS' HALL – where the servants ate their meals and spent any spare time. Its sparse furniture included two deal tables and benches, an old cupboard, and a couple of beds.

The LAUNDRY – where the laundry was rinsed, starched, dried, pressed and ironed (it was actually washed in a WASHHOUSE containing three coppers outside in the yard)

The basement also contains the Duchess of Lauderdale's private BATHROOM which is connected by a hidden staircase to her apartment above. In the 1670s, this was an extremely unusual and advanced amenity. Very few English houses had bathrooms before the nineteenth century.

Note the PATTYPANS hanging from the shelf, the ROLLING PIN, the man putting a pie into the oven with a PEEL, and the rush mats under the pies.

Abraham Bosse (1602–1676), French print, c. 1640.

# The SERVANTS

THE HOUSEHOLD ACCOUNT BOOKS for Ham House show that there were about twenty servants on the payroll in the 1670s. The number of servants fluctuated according to the time of year (hiring took place each quarter) and whether the Duke and Duchess of Lauderdale were in residence. When they were away a skeleton staff was left in charge of Ham House on 'board wages'. The following list of servants from the household account book for 1668 is particularly interesting because it gives their annual wages:

Ham House overlooks the River Thames. The fish basket illustrated in this picture was reproduced for the kitchen.

Wenceslaus Hollar (1607–1677), print, c. 1650.

| | | | |
|---|---|---|---|
| The Chaplain | £30.00 | The waighting gentlewoman | £10.00 |
| The stuart (steward) | £20.00 | The housekeeper | £ 8.00 |
| The page | — | The chambermaid | £ 5.00 |
| The butler | £ 6.00 | The children's maid | £ 4.00 |
| The coachman | £ 6.00 | The landry (laundry) maid | £ 4.00 |
| The cooke | £20.00 | The landry (laundry) maid | £ 4.00 |
| The footman | £ 7.00 | The hous maid | £ 4.00 |
| The groom | £ 6.00 | The hous maid | £ 3.10 |
| The postillion | £ 4.00 | The dary (dairy) maid | £ 3.10 |
| | | The scullery maid | £ 3.10 |

## INTRODUCTION *to the* seventeenth-century KITCHEN *and* LARDER *at* HAM

THE KITCHEN and its adjacent larder are being restored to their appearance on a typical June/July day of the 1670s, when the Duke and Duchess of Lauderdale were in residence. (They were constantly on the move between their establishments at Ham, Windsor, Whitehall and Bath.)

During their ten years of marriage (1672–82), Ham House became one of the most lavishly furnished and up-to-date homes in England. The kitchen boasted all the latest technology and equipment. Few other kitchens at this time were furnished with a mechanical *spit-jack* to turn the spit in front of the fire, a charcoal-burning brick *stewing stove* for cooking delicate stews and sauces, or an iron *range* with a moveable 'cheek' or side, a convenience which allowed the cook to make up a large or small fire as required.

## What's going on *in the* KITCHEN?

A large brass pot is hanging over the coal fire in the range. Beef is simmering away inside the pot beneath the wooden lid.

John Blangy, the cook, has just put some pullets on to a spit to roast in front of the fire. He has gone off to the scullery to fetch an iron dripping pan which goes below the birds to collect their fat. (The pan was dirty and had to be scrubbed out with sand and water.)

On the left hob of the fire, a cake is rising underneath a flannel cloth.

The charcoal is soon to be lit in the stewing stove so that a sauce can be prepared for the pullets. The stove has no flue, so the window above it has to be opened to get rid of the noxious fumes.

The large central table is laid for the servants' meal. John Blangy and his two kitchen maids, Mary Trever and Grace Phyllipps, will have some of the broth from the beef pot as well as the roast chicken and bread already on the table. The broth will be served in pewter porringers and eaten with pewter spoons. They will eat the chicken with their fingers off wooden trenchers.

A woman carrying a VEGETABLE BASKET and wearing PATTENS to keep her shoes dry. These ephemeral objects were reproduced for the kitchen.

Wenceslaus Hollar (1607–1677), print dated 1640.

There is a cabbage in a string net on the central table, waiting to go into the pot hanging over the fire. Once the cabbage is cooked, the net is fished out with a fork.

There is a large rinsing tub of water on the table too. Some strawberries and mushrooms have just been washed in it, drained in the earthenware colander, and left to dry on a linen cloth.

On the dresser to the left, some almonds are being pounded in the marble mortar with a lignum vitae pestle.

An assortment of pies has just come back from the bake-house and has been laid out on the dresser to the right. The pie shaped like a fish contains a whole salmon caught in the Thames early this morning. The fruit tart with the openwork top has a quince and pear filling and is decorated with candied orange, lemon peel and coriander. The enormous scallop-shaped 'bride' pie has six different fillings, one of which (a live snake, as a joke!) is still to come. The rest of the pies contain rich mixtures of meat, fruit and spices. In most cases, pastry was not meant to be eaten in the seventeenth century : it simply provided an inexpensive and decorative 'coffin' for cooking the filling without losing its flavour and moisture.

In the passageway connecting the kitchen to the courtyard outside, there is a tub of rubbish which cannot be burned in the kitchen range, some fresh food delivered by estate workers and local tradesmen and a pair of pattens, a kind of raised over-shoe, worn for wet work like mopping the kitchen floor or for trips out of doors in wet weather.

The CUPBOARD for storing food is similar to that in the kitchen. The simple KITCHEN CHAIR with its rush seat was used as a model for reproduction.
Wenceslaus Hollar (1607–1677), *Aesop's Fables*, London, 1655.

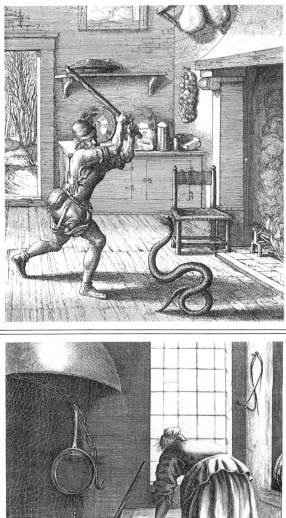

This picture was used as a model in recreating the larder. It shows how foods were laid out on DRESSER TABLES and SHELVES or suspended from nails.
Wenceslaus Hollar (1607–1677), *Aesop's Fables*, London, 1665.

Reproductions were made of the GRIDIRON (for broiling meat and fish) and FIRE TONGS. The adjustable POT HANGER on the right gripped the sides of a cooking pot.
Geertruyt Rogman (active c. 1647–1658), Dutch print, mid seventeenth-century.

The man on the KITCHEN CHAIR is sweeping ashes with a HEARTH BRUSH. Note the 'KETTLE' suspended over the fire from a CHAIN and POT HOOK.
Jan Luyken (1649–1712), *Het Leerzam Huisraad*, Amsterdam, 1711.

# The Official List

of contents *of the* kitchen *and* larder *at* HAM HOUSE,
*collated from the inventories of 1677, 1679 and 1683*
*(the list is presented in alphabetical order, with original spellings)*:

## The KITCHEN

1 tin APPLE ROASTER
1 copper BASKET
1 copper BASIN
1 pair of BELLOWS
2 iron CANDLESTICKS
3 CHAIRS
1 leather CHAIR
2 CLEAVERS
2 COLANDERS (at least one being brass)
1 COPPER TO BOIL MEAT
   iron serving DISHES
7 stewing DISHES
4 brass DISHES for servants' meat
2 copper DISHES for meat
2 tin DREDGING BOXES
4 DRESSER-BOARDS
1 FENDER
1 FLOUR BOX
1 fire FORK
1 flesh of beef FORK
1 FORM
1 iron GRATE with sliding check
1 tin GRATER
2 GRIDIRONS
1 JACK with three chains
1 brass water KETTLE
1 fish KETTLE and false bottom
2 chopping KNIVES
3 mincing KNIVES
1 brass basting LADLE
1 brass LADLE
12 brass LARDING PINS
1 brass MORTAR with an iron PESTLE
2 marble MORTARS with PESTLES
1 stone MORTAR with wooden PESTLE
1 brass PAIL
1 PAIRING SHOVEL [a wooden,

spade-like implement for
dividing a large quantity of
'proven' dough into loaf-sized
pieces]
1 large carp PAN and COVER,
   with false bottom
2 iron dripping PANS
3 frying PANS
9 saucePANS
6 stewing PANS
4 PATTYPANS with 3 COVERS and
   2 sets of PATTYPANS [small
   round tins for baking pies]
12 PATTEITS [very small tins for
   baking individual pies in
   different shapes and forms]
   PEWTER: PLATES, DISHES and MAZARINES
2 pastry PEELS
2 POT HOOKS
5 brass POTS and 4 COVERS
1 pair iron RACKS
2 iron RINGS
1 ROWLING PIN
2 SHELVES
1 fire SHOVEL
2 SKIMMERS
1 SPICE BOX
6 SPITS
9 lark SPITS
1 brass SPOON
1 iron STAND
1 TOASTING IRON
   TONGS
1 wooden TRAY
9 iron TRIVETS
3 TUBS (1 for rinsing, 1 for salt
and 1 for flour)

## The LARDER

1 vinegar BARRILL
2 BASKETTS
2 DRESSER BOARDS
1 leather CHAYRE
1 pair of iron beam SCALES and WEIGHTS
1 lead SISTERN

1 STOOL TO KILL HOGS ON
2 beefe TUBS
1 flour TUB
2 powdering TUBBS with COVERS
1 TUB for eggs
1 TUB to salt bacon in

# What can you see *in the* LARDER?

A small selection of the many foods eaten during the months of June and July and some 'left-overs'.

A stool to kill hogs on and cut up their carcases.

A vinegar barrel with a tap at the bottom.

A mouse caught in a trap.

A delivery of different kinds of sugar from London. Sugar came in several forms in the seventeenth century. On the shelf there are two large sugar cones weighing 15 lbs each and two small ones weighing 2 lbs each. These have to be broken up before use: small pieces are then pounded in a mortar and sieved to get rid of remaining lumps. In the brown sacks on the floor there are more expensive kinds of sugar: '*white sugar candy*' (irregular large white crystals); '*earthed*' or '*white powder sugar*' (grey granulated sugar); '*royal*' or *double refined sugar*' (looks like coarse white salt); '*brown sugar candy*' (not unlike our modern brown sugar crystals); '*refined*' sugar (resembling uncooked tapioca); *brown sugar* (like ours); and '*muscovado*' or crude dark brown sugar. White, highly refined sugar was the most expensive kind in the 1670s and brown sugar the cheapest.

# How *the* KITCHEN *and* LARDER *were restored*

WHEN RESTORATION WORK started in the kitchen, all that remained from the 1670s was the central table (probably built with the house in 1610), the dresser and shelves to the right, a large white marble mortar, hearth brush and iron fireback. Although the dresser with cupboards below it (to the left) is seventeenth-century in design, it was probably installed at the end of the eighteenth century, when large storage drawers were added to the central table and dresser. The larder next door was completely bare.

Fortunately, there is a great deal of information about domestic life at Ham in the seventeenth century which has made it possible to restore the kitchen and larder to their appearance on a typical June/July day of the 1670s. The most important sources of information are:

# *List*

of the cheap, ephemeral items *in the* kitchen *and* larder *enumerated in the* household account books *and/or* seventeenth-century cookery books

*(in alphabetical order and modern spelling)*

APPLE SCOOP
BASKETS
BASINS
BEER CAN (wooden)
BOTTLES, made out of glass and earthenware
BOWLS
BROOMS
BRUSHES
CABBAGE NETS
CHAFING DISH
DRINKING CUPS or POTS
EARTHEN PANS
FIRKINS (for pottage) [a firkin was a small cask, a quarter the size of a barrel, used for storing liquids or foods like butter and fish]
GALLY POTS and WINGS [galley pots are small earthen glazed pots; wings could be birds' wings, which were used as brushes]
GLASSES
GLAZING IRON
GOOSE QUILLS and HEN'S FEATHERS for brushing egg yolk onto pastry
HEARTH BRUSH
KITCHEN PAPER
KNIFE for opening oysters
LADLES (wooden)
MOP
MOUSE TRAP
MUG
MUSTARD POT
NUTCRACKER

PACK THREAD
PATTENS
PIGGINS [a small wooden pail, with one stave left longer than the others to serve as a handle]
PIPKINS
PLATTERS (wooden)
PORRINGERS
POTS, made out of earthenware, for storing food and pickles, usually covered in bladders to keep out the air
PRESERVING GLASSES
RUBBING BRUSH
RUSHES for pricking food
SALTS, wooden and pewter
SCISSORS
SIEVE (made out of hair)
SILIBUB POT
SKILLET FRAMES
SPILLS for lighting the range, stewing stove, candles etc.
SPOONS (wooden)
TEA CUPS and POT
TEXTILES [e.g. aprons for servants, flannel cloth for covering rising dough, white linen table cloth, dish cloths, linen cloths for drying vegetables and fruit, hand towels, tiffany bag, boulter cloth, pudding cloth, dresser cloths etc.]
TINDER BOX
TRENCHERS (wooden)
WHISK

1. INVENTORIES made in the years 1677, 1679 and 1683 which list all the most valuable contents of the two rooms. These inventories were collated to produce an 'official' list of objects (see box 1, p.14).

2. MANUSCRIPT HOUSEHOLD ACCOUNT BOOKS which itemize every object bought for Ham House (however humble) and reveal exactly what food and drink the household was consuming each week and what it cost.

3. SEVENTEENTH-CENTURY COOKERY BOOKS which provide much useful information about the utensils and equipment needed to follow the 'receipts' fashionable at the time. For example, seventeenth-century recipes clearly expect cooks to have several means of straining food at their disposal: coarse or fine lawn cloths, hair sieves, jelly bags, strainers made out of tiffany or cushion canvas, and both earthen and metal colanders. Yet the only type of strainer to appear in the 'official' inventory is a brass colander. The cheap, ephemeral items bought for the kitchen and larder which are enumerated in the household account books and/or mentioned in seventeenth-century cookery books are listed in box 2 opposite.

4. SEVENTEENTH-CENTURY BOOK ILLUSTRATIONS, PRINTS, DRAWINGS AND PAINTINGS which help to show what different objects looked like and how rooms were arranged.

So far as possible genuine seventeenth-century objects are shown in the kitchen and larder. In some cases, however, these could not be found in good condition or at the right price; and in many other cases, the items that were originally present simply have not survived. Things like kitchen paper, birch whisks for whipping egg whites, tin cheese graters, baskets, dish cloths, tubs and barrels simply do not stand up to 300 years of wear. Rather than omitting these items altogether, which would give a misleading impression, a number of specialist workers were commissioned to make faithful reproductions of them. Some of the seventeenth-century pictures used as models in the restoration of the kitchen and larder are reproduced in this book.

# What kinds *of* FOODS *were* eaten?

THE FOLLOWING LIST of foodstuffs consumed at Ham, Windsor, London and Bath between 1668 and 1677 has been compiled from manuscript books of domestic disbursements kept for Elizabeth, Countess of Dysart and (after 1672) for the Duke and Duchess of Lauderdale. Most of the food came from specialist suppliers. (The butcher, the fishmonger, the poulterer, the baker, the grocer, the brewer, the aleman and the vintner are all named.) Vegetables and herbs were bought from the gardener. Seasonal delicacies often came from local people eager to make a little money or curry favour, or from tenant farmers who could not manage all their rent in cash.

It is often thought that the well to do in the seventeenth century ate enormous quantities of meat and few fruit and vegetables. (This is partly because contemporary accounts of feasts concentrate on the meat served and partly because seventeenth-century cookery books devote rather little space to fruits and vegetables.) However, the list of food given below shows that this was not true of the Lauderdales. Contemporary spellings are given and food prices are indicated when it is possible to work them out.

## *A*

AILL (i.e. ail, the awn or husk of barley)

ALE (cost anything from 1d to 2d a pint; it was sold in bottles containing 2–3 pints, in barrels, and by the quart)

ALMONDS (varied in price from 1s 4d to 1s 9d a pound; 'Jordan' almonds are sometimes specified)

AMBER (a local name for the plant, Tutsan; its leaves, when dried, smell sharp and aromatic like ambergris)

AMBER (ambergris) and *Musk* (both were used for perfuming food and were important ingredients in confectionery)

ANCHOVIES (1s–2s a pound)

ANISEED (1d an ounce)

APPLES (the different varieties bought include *Codlings, Golden Pippins, John Apples, Mounser Johns, Pippins, Runnets or Rennets, Russolins, and Wardons;* they were usually bought in large quantities, i.e. by the bushel or by the hundred; the price of a dozen apples ranged from $2\frac{1}{2}$d–6d)

APRICOTS (a dozen cost about 1s 6d)

AQUA VITAE (strong spirits such as brandy; 1 gallon cost 2s 8d)

ARTICHOKES (both fresh and pickled artichokes were bought; an artichoke was cheapest in September (3d) and most expensive in January (10d))

This is a very grand, well equipped Italian kitchen from the second half of the sixteenth-century. Many culinary innovations adopted in England came from Italy and France.

G.G. Valegio (c. 1548–1587), print, c. 1580.

# ℬ

BACON (cost 9d a pound all the year round)

BARBERRIES (1 gallon cost 1s 3d)

BAR CODS (probably cod, the fish)

BARLEY (French barley, pearl barley, wheat barley are sometimes specified; it cost from 5d–10d a pound)

BAYS (bay leaves; also called *laurel*)

BEANS (3s 1d a bushel)

BEAN FLOWERS

BEEF (including *smoked beef*; this cost about 1s 6d a pound)

BEER

BERYAMINE (?)

BISCUITS (the term included small cakes; they weighed about $2\frac{1}{2}$ oz each and cost between 1s 2d and 1s 8d a pound)

BLACK PUDDING

BRANDY (6d to 8d a pint)

BREAD (*stale bread, wheat bread for puddings, white bread for puddings, French rolls* and *white penny bread* are sometimes singled out in the accounts)

BROOM BUDS (broom is a shrub bearing yellow flowers; a quart cost 2s)

BULLIES (bullaces, wild plums; in season in October and November)

BUTTER (cost 4d–8d a pound depending on its quality; ordinary, fresh, salt and sweet butter are all mentioned)

The kitchen

The kitchen

# C

CABBAGES (usually bought with carrots and turnips; Savoy cabbages are sometimes specified)

CALVES CHALDRON (entrails)

CALVES FEET (often bought with tripe, hogs' ears, sheep's trotters and cow heels; 2 pairs of calves' feet cost 1s)

CALVES HEAD (cost 1s 6d–2s 10d)

CALVES SWEETBREADS

CANDIED CITREON (candied lemon or lime; half a pound cost 1s 6d)

CANDIED LEMON

CANDIED ORANGES (half a pound cost 1s)

CAPERS (1s a pound)

CAPONS (the average capon weighed 2½ lbs and cost 2s 6d)

CARDOONS (a vegetable similar to artichoke; grown for its celery-like stalks; usually bought with herbs and endives)

CARPS (2s per fish)

CARROTS (invariably bought with turnips and cabbages)

CARROWAY COMFITS (carroway flavoured sweets; 1s 4d–1s 6d a pound)

CARROWAY SEEDS (1s 3d–1s 6d a pound)

CAULIFLOWER (6d a head)

CELERY

CHEESE (large quantities of cheese were bought; the kind of cheese is not usually specified but *Cheshire cheese, Cream cheese, Mild Cheese, New Milk Cheese, Suffolk Cheese* and *Thin Cheese* are sometimes named; the price varied from 1d to 4½d a pound)

CHEESE CURDS

CHERRIES (in season during May, June and July; the eight varieties available were called *Black, Carnation, Duke, Flemish, Hart, May, Morello,* and *White Cristal Hart*; their price fluctuated wildly from 1½d to 5s a pound)

CHESTNUTS (1s–1s 6d a pound)

CHICKENS (the price of a chicken varied from 4d to 1s 4d depending on weight; 'cramb' or 'crambed' chickens are sometimes specified; these would have been forcefed)

CINNOMAN (7d an ounce)

CITREON (2s to 5s a pound; cf. the entry for *Candied Citreon* above)

CLOVES (1s an ounce)

COCK (bought for making 'broth' or stock and cost from 1s 6d to 1s 9d each)

COCKS COMBS (the crests of cocks or cockerels were often used as a decorative garnish)

CODS HEAD

COFFEE (2s 6d a pound; it could be bought ready ground)

COLEWORTS (any plant of the cabbage family; these were usually bought with sprouts or spinage which suggests that they were cooked in combination)

Pictures of 'Butchery', 'Cookery', 'Metals' and 'Fire', from an illustrated Latin textbook.

Johann Comenius (1592–1670), *Orbis Sensualium Pictus*, first published in Nuremberg in 1658. It was translated from German into English by Charles Hoole and published in London in 1689.

COMFITTS (comfits, sweetmeats made out of a fruit or root preserved with sugar; they cost 6d a pound)

CORDIAL WATER, *ingredients to make* (this was supposed to invigorate the heart and stimulate the circulation)

CORIANDER SEEDS (1d an ounce)

COCHINEAL (a scarlet dye made out of the dried bodies of an insect found on certain species of Mexican cactus)

COW HEEL (usually bought with tripe and sheeps trotters)

COWSLIP FLOWERS (half a peck cost 7d)

CRABS (10d each)

CRAY FISH or *Craw Fish* (100 cost from 3s 6d to 4s)

CREAM (6d a pint)

CUCUMBER

CUMIN SEEDS (1d a pound)

CURRANTS (*dried currants*, i.e. raisins prepared from seedless grapes, cost 6d a pound; *fresh white currants* cost 1d a pint)

# D

DAMSONS (1½d to 2d a pint)

DUCKLINGS (1s 6d each)

DUCKS (cost from 5d to 1s 8d each, according to weight; the average *salted duck* cost 1s 1d)

# E

EELS (from 10d to 2s 9d each)

EGGS (5s per hundred)

ENDIVES (usually bought with herbs, lettuce, watercress and horseradish)

EPSUM WATER (mineral water from a spring at Epsom in Surrey; it cost 5d a bottle)

ERINGO ROOTS (sea holly roots were eaten pickled or candied; they cost 1s 6d per half pound)

# F

FAGGOTS (a quart consisting of a hundred faggots cost 2s 6d)

FELLFARE (fieldfare, a species of thrush, costing 2d each)

FIGS

FLOUNDERS (2d each)

FLOWER (flour, half a peck of fine flour cost 1s 3d)

FLOUR ROLLS (5 dozen cost 5s)

FRUIT (the kinds bought 'for the table' were not always specified)

GAMMON

GEESE (cost anything from 1s to 3s 6d each; young geese were called either *green geese* or *goslings* and cost from 1s 1d to 2s each)

GELLATINE (gelatine)

GERKINS (200 small ones cost 4s)

GINGER (half a pound cost 6d)

GOOSEBERRIES (in season from April through July and cost 1d to 1½d a pint)

GOUGEONS or *godgeons* (gudgeons, small freshwater fish)

GRAPES (in season from September to November and cost 2s a basket)

HARE (1s 10d to 2s 4d each)

HARTSHORNE (hartshorn is the horn or antler of a hart, a source of ammonia; the shavings were used to make an edible jelly; it cost from 1s 8d to 2s 6d a pound)

HERBS (bought throughout the year)

HERRINGS (these cost ½d each; *red herrings* are sometimes specified)

HOGS (between September and January; a whole one might cost £1 19s 4½d; the cuts of the animal also bought include *Hogs Cheek*, *Hogs Ears*, *Hogs Foot* and *Hogs Gutts*)

HONEY

HOPS (in June, July and August; these cost 7d to 8d a pound)

HORSERADISH (usually bought with herbs, endives, lettuce, savoy cabbages, bay leaves and rosemary)

## I

JUNIPER BERRIES (cost 6d a pound)

JUNIPER WATER (sold by the quart or the bottle and usually cost 1s 6d a pint)

## L

LAMB (a whole lamb cost 10s to 16s; however, it was usually bought by the quarter or side; *Lambs Heads* were also bought)

LAMPES (lampreys, primitive fish somewhat like eels)

LANTEALE (probably lentils; they cost 2s 6d a pound)

LARD (8d a pound)

LARKS (eaten in December, January and February; 5 dozen cost 6s)

LATTICE (lettuce; invariably bought with endives, herbs, horseradish or watercress)

LEMONS (bought throughout the year, usually with oranges; a dozen could cost as little as 1s or as much as 3s, depending on the month)

The BASKET in this picture was reproduced. Fish were often caught in the nearby River Thames and brought to the kitchen to be cooked.

Wenceslaus Hollar (1607–1677), print.

LIQUORISH (liquorice)
LOBSTER (1s 6d)

# *M*

MACE (1s an ounce)
MACKAROONS (macaroons)
MACKERELS (2d each)
MALT (a peck cost from 10d to 1s)
MAROONS (a large kind of sweet chestnut; 200 cost 3s)
MARROW BONES
MEAL (5s a bushel)
MILK
MILK WATER (2s a bottle)
MORILLES (morels, an edible fungus)
MULBERRIES (in season from July to September; sold by the basket or the quart)
MULLET (2s each)
MUSHROOMS

MUSK (bought with ambergris and cinnamon)
MUSMELLONS (a kind of melon?; bought in August)
MUSTARD (a pot of mustard cost 4d)
MUSTARD SEED
MUTTON (cuts specified include the side, hind quarter, breast and neck, leg, shoulder)

# N

NEATS FEET (the feet of an ox, bullock, cow or heifer; they were often bought in pairs, with tripe or sheep's trotters)
NEATS TONGUE (ox tongue; cost 1s 4d to 3s each; sometimes bought with a *Neats Udder*)
NECTARINES (2 dozen cost 6s)
NUTMEG (2s 8d for 4 ounces)

# O

OATMEAL (4s to 6s a bushel)
OIL (for salads; cost 1s a pint)
OLIVES (ordinary olives cost 6d a pint; but Lule Olives cost 11d a pint)
ONIONS
ORANGES (bought throughout the year, often with lemons; their price fluctuated from 1s to 2s 2d a dozen; *Candied Orange, Orange Flowers, Orange Peel,* and *Orange Schips* or chips were also bought)
OX (an *Ox Cheek* cost 9d; an *Ox Tongue* cost 1s 6d, often with an OX PALATE thrown in too)
OYSTERS (bought by the barrel, the pint, the quart and the hundred; cost 1s a pint)

# P

PALATES (the roof of a cow or ox's mouth; often bought with sweetbreads and ox tongue; cost 2d each)
PARSLEY ROOTS
PARSNIPS (bought with carrots, turnips and cabbages)
PARTRIDGES (eaten in both summer and winter; a pair in January might cost anything from 2s 6d to 3s 6d)
PEACHES (in season from July to October; 2 dozen might cost as much as 8s; *Nerwinton* peaches are sometimes specified)
PEARS (many different kinds of pear were bought: *Pearmains* in January and February; *Windsor Pears* at 1s to 2s a dozen in July and August; *Burgundy Pears* and *Catherin Pears* in September and October; *Baking Pears* in October; and in December a box of *Dryed Pears* at £1 6s, *French Bonchitian Pears* at 13 for 15s and *Pearmains*)

The larder

Ham House

Liquids (e.g. beer, vinegar) and solids (e.g. salted meat, flour, mustard, pickled vegetables) were transported and stored in barrels and casks such as these.

Anonymous painting of Broad Quay, Bristol, c. 1728.

PEARCHES (perch)

PEAS (bought by the sack or the peck ; white peas are sometimes specified)

PEAS TOPS (bought with herbs)

PEPPER (2s a pound; white pepper is sometimes specified at 2s 2d a pound)

PHEASANTS (eaten in summer as well as winter; cost from 2s to 3s 8d each)

PIG (from 1s 8d to 5s each)

PIGEONS (eaten the whole year round; a distinction was drawn between tame and wild birds, the former costing about 9d each and the latter $3\frac{1}{2}$d)

PIKE (2s to 2s 9d each)

PISTACHIO NUTS (from 1s 8d to 2s a pound)

PLAGUE WATER (a kind of medicine supposed to ward off the plague; 6s a quart)

PLOVER (a kind of bird ; 1s 6d each)

PLUMS (the 13 different varieties mentioned include *amber, apricot, black pear, cristal, damson, French, French sugar, great Mogul, imperial, mussel, pear, white pare and white*; they were sold by the pint, the dozen or the hundred and were in season from July to October with French sugar plums being bought in December)

POMECITRON PEEL (citron peel)

POMEGRANATE (pomegranites; 11 cost 8s in December)

PRAWNS (usually bought in April, May, June and July; cost 1s 3d a pint)

PRUNES (bought in winter; cost 2s a pound)

PULLETS (1s 2d to 2s each)

# Q

QUAIL (bought in June, with turkeys)

QUINCES (in season from October to December; cost 1s 4d to 4s a dozen)

# R

RABBITS (bought throughout the year; cost from 7d to 11d each)

RAISINS (bought in winter; ordinary raisins cost 3d a pound, *Malaga raisins* 3½d a pound and *Raisins Solis*, i.e. of the sun, 5d a pound)

RASBERRIES (i.e. raspberries; in season in July; 3d a pint)

RICE (4d a pound)

ROOTS (bought with herbs)

ROSES (the petals were used in cooking as well as for decoration; they were bought in June and July; 'blowed' roses 'red roses' and 'red rose buds' are all specified)

ROSE WATER

ROSEMARY (usually bought with bay leaves, horseradish and herbs)

RYE (a bushel cost 3s 2d)

# S

SACK (1s a pint)

SAFFRON

ST JOHNSWORT (St John's Wort, the herb Greater Celandine, also known as 'salatin' or 'saladine')

SALLET (salad materials)

SALMON (2 salmon cost 17s)

SALT (bought throughout the year and cost from 2s 8d to 3s 6d a bushel; *bay salt* and *white salt* were also bought)

SALT FISH (bought in summer as well as winter)

SAMPHIRE (a herb which grows by the sea; eaten pickled or in salad; it cost 6d a pound)

SAUSAGES (cost 8d a pound; 'Bullonia' or Bologna sausages are sometimes specified)

SHEEP (a sheep weighing 5 stone cost 13s; the different cuts of sheep bought regularly include *Sheeps Head*, *Sheeps Paunch*, *Sheeps Trotters*, *Sheeps Tongue*)

SHRIMPS (1s a pint)

SHRUB (a drink made out of citrus fruits and spirits; 3s a bottle)
SKERRETS (skirrets, a root vegetable eaten in winter)
SMELTS (250 cost 1s 2d)
SNIPE (small birds eaten in winter)
SOLE (bought with whiting)
SOW (a sow and her young pigs cost £1 19s)
SPARROW GRASS (asparagus; bought from December through to May; 100 cost anything from 1s to 5s)
SPINNAGE (spinage; always bought with horseradish and colewort)
SPROUTS (in season from January through May; invariably bought with cabbage)
STRAWBERRIES (in season in June; a basket cost 1s)
SUET (3d to 6d a pound)
SUGAR (see the larder section above for a summary of the different types of sugar used in the late seventeenth century; a 4 lb loaf of sugar cost 3s 4d; a pound of double refined sugar is 1s 6d; a pound of brown sugar 5d)
SWEETBREADS
SYRUP OF VIOLET (10s a quart)

*T*

TEAL (small duck; 3 cost 4s)
THORNBACK (common ray or skate; 1s 5d per fish)
TONGUE (1s 6d each)
TREACLE (a pound of London treacle cost 2s 8d)
TRIPE (invariably bought with sheep's trotters, neats' feet, cow heels, calves' feet, or hogs' feet)
TROUT (1s 6d each)
TURBOT (1s 9d each)
TURKEYS (from 4s 6d to 6s each)
TURNIPS (often bought with carrots and cabbages)

*U*

UDDERS (1s 1d each)

*V*

VEAL (cuts specified include *hind quarter, quarter, leg, side*)
VERMIZOLI (probably *vermicelli*, a kind of *pasta*; it was added to soups)
VIOLETS (the flowers were candied, made into cakes and turned into paste, syrup and oil; 6d a quart)
VINEGAR (3d a pint; beer vinegar cost 1d a pint)
VINE WATER

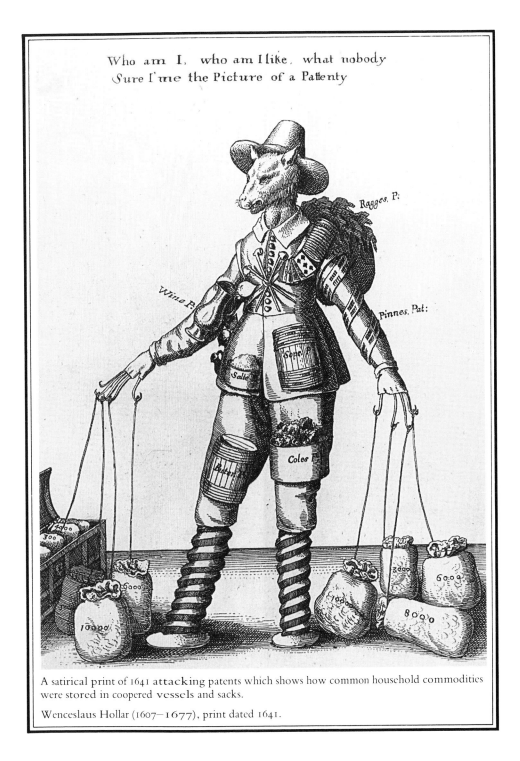

A satirical print of 1641 attacking patents which shows how common household commodities were stored in coopered vessels and sacks.

Wenceslaus Hollar (1607—1677), print dated 1641.

#  W

WALNUTS (in season in September and October; 8d per hundred)

WATER (see entry under Epsum water)

WATERCRESS (usually bought with herbs and roots)

WAFERS (described as 'sheet wafers')

WESTFALIA HAM (Westphalia ham; 3 hams weighing 28½ lbs cost £1 8s 6d)

WHEAT (rod wheat is sometimes specified)

WHEATEAR (a small bird)

WHEY (a quart cost 4d)

WHITING (12 cost from 10d to 1s 6d)

WILD FOWL

WINE (*Canary, Claret, Burgundy,* and *white wine* are all specified; it was sold by the bottle, pint, gallon and hogshead)

WOODCOCK (a small bird costing from 1s 6d to 2s 6d each)

# Y

YEAST

Some typical shapes of seventeenth-century JUGS and
BELLARMINE POTS.
Wenceslaus Hollar (1607–1677), *Aesop's Fables*,
London, 1665.

A woman puts meat on to a SPIT while a child turns
another over the DRIPPING PAN. Note the POT over the fire
and quantity of PEWTER on display.     Wenceslaus Hollar
(1607–1677), *Aesop's Fables*, London, 1665.

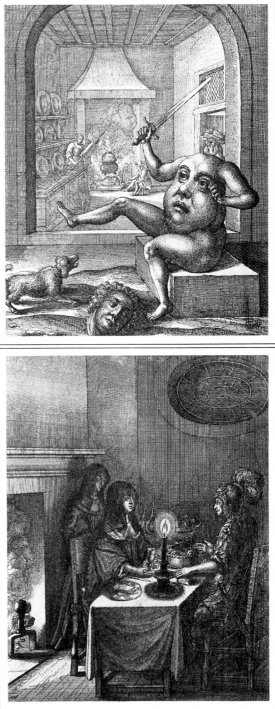

The BIRD BASKET and EGG BASKET were reproduced for
the kitchen.
Wenceslaus Hollar (1607–1677), English print, c. 1660.

A seventeenth-century woman dining with an imaginary
warrior.
Wenceslaus Hollar (1607–1677), English print, c. 1660.

See how the plates, trenchers and knives are arranged geometrically, like the garden glimpsed out of the window. The FRUIT BASKETS were copied for the kitchen.

Wenceslaus Hollar (1607–1677), English print dated 1659.

# Meals *at* HAM HOUSE

FOOD PREPARED in the kitchen, bake-house, still-house and dairy and wine and beer stored in the cellars were assembled in the BUTTERY to the right of the entrance hall on the ground floor, before being served at table. When the Duke and Duchess were *en famille* they ate in the MARBLE DINING ROOM near the buttery, which could accommodate twelve to eighteen people sitting at two or three oval 'gate-leg' tables. (See room 2, which now has a wooden parquet floor.) But when entertaining, the Lauderdales ate in the more ceremonious GREAT DINING ROOM on the first floor which had seating for eighteen. (See room 17.)

The late seventeenth-century dining-table was covered with a starched white cloth and laid with dishes and table decorations in formal, geometric patterns rather like a garden. It was not uncommon to raise the central dishes on boards concealed below the table cloth to create a tiered effect and elaborate pyramids of fruit, jellies and sweetmeats were very popular as centrepieces. In spring and summer flower petals were often scattered on the table cloth to look pretty and smell nice. The Duchess of Lauderdale had a large collection of plate and each guest was equipped with a matching spoon, fork and knife, a trencher to eat off and a tumbler to drink from.

Some typical table plans drawn up by Charles Carter 'lately cook to his Grace the Duke of Argyll, the Earl of Pontefract, the Lord Cornwallis, etc.' in *The Complete Practical Cook: or, a New System of the whole Art and Mystery of Cookery* (1730) are reproduced on pages 40 and 41. They show how symmetrically the dishes were laid out on the table.

Two to three courses were served at dinner (the main meal of the day which began at 2 o'clock), with anything from six to twenty-five different dishes per course. The first course consisted mainly of boiled or roasted meat with a little broth or soup, a few boiled savoury puddings, and meaty pies and pasties. The second course was basically a repeat of the first course with the addition of roasted birds, poached fish and seafood, salads, pickles, and sweet creams, custards and fruit pies. The third course was devoted to sweet things: fresh fruit (if in season), preserved fruit, conserves, sweetmeats, biscuits and cakes.

Some suggestions for 'bills of fare' suitable for June and July are provided by Patrick Lamb, master cook to Charles II, James II, and William and Mary, in *Royal Cookery; or, the Complete Court Cook* (1710). These are given overleaf with brief explanations. It is worth noting that most of the suggested dishes were part of the standard seventeenth-century culinary repertoire and relatively simple to prepare. Patrick Lamb only provides recipes in his book for his personal specialities (these are marked with an asterisk).

# For June

## FIRST COURSE

ROASTED PIKE AND SMELTS
*[ the fish was spit-roasted in front of the fire ]*

WESTPHALIA HAM* AND YOUNG FOWLS
*[ the ham was first pickled in salt, salt-petre, brown sugar and water for three weeks and then smoked up the chimney for 10 days; the young fowls would probably have been spit-roasted in front of the fire ]*

MARROW PUDDING*
*[ a pudding containing bread crumbs, milk, minced bone marrow, nutmeg, rosewater and almonds which was boiled in skins made out of ox or hog guts ]*

HAUNCH OF VENISON ROASTED

RAGOO OF LAMB-STONES AND SWEETBREADS
*[ a stew made out of lamb's testicles and sweetbreads with a highly flavoured sauce thickened with fried flour ]*

FRICASEE OF YOUNG RABBETS ETC.
*[ a stew made out of boiling rabbits in broth or stewing slices of rabbit meat in butter, adding liquid, and thickening the resulting sauce with eggs or flour ]*

UMBLE PYES
*[ pies made out of the entrails of a deer, i.e. its heart, liver etc. ]*

DISH OF MULLETS

ROASTED FOWLS

DISH OF CUSTARDS
*[ open pies filled with an egg and milk mixture ]*

## SECOND COURSE

DISH OF YOUNG PHEASANTS

DISH OF FRY'D SOLES AND EELS

POTATO-PYE
*[ this was sweetened with sugar ]*

JOLE OF STURGEON
*[ head and shoulders of sturgeon ]*

DISH OF TARTS AND CHEESECAKES

DISH OF FRUIT OF SORTS

SULLEBUBS
*[ syllabubs ]*

# *For July*

## FIRST COURSE

COCK SALMON, WITH BUTTER'D LOBSTER

DISH OF SCOTCH-COLLOPS
*[ thin slices of salted mutton or beef broiled over a gridiron and served with vinegar and butter ]*

CHINE OF VEAL
*[ the backbone, with its adjoining flesh ]*

VENISON-PASTY
*[ venison pie ]*

GRAND SALLAD
*[ this could take three forms: (1) a selection of pickles laid out neatly in a dish with a small tree or ornament in the middle; (2) a selection of soused meats, cut in slices; (3) a selection of coloured jellies ]*

ROASTED GEESE AND DUCKLINGS

PATTY ROYAL
*[ a little pie or pasty with a rich filling ]*

ROASTED PIG LARDED
*[ strips of fat were inserted into the meat before spit-roasting ]*

STEW'D CARPS

DISH OF CHICKENS BOIL'D WITH BACON, ETC.

## SECOND COURSE

DISH OF PARTRIDGES AND QUAILS

DISH OF LOBSTERS AND PRAWNS

DISH OF DUCKS AND TAME PIGEONS

DISH OF JELLYS
*[ these were made by boiling calves' or neats' feet in water and adding sugar, wine or sack, beaten egg whites, spices, colourings etc. ]*

DISH OF FRUIT

DISH OF MARINATED FISH
*[ the fish was first fried in oil and then pickled in a mixture of wine, vinegar, sweet herbs, lemon peel and spices ]*

DISH OF TARTS OF SORTS
*[ these would have had fruit fillings ]*

# A dinner for the King, Jany 7th

Side    Board

To Change    To Change

A Collar of Brawn

A Chine of Bacon & Turkey    A Chine of Beef

A Ham Rost & Pullets    A Venison Pasty

A Pulpatoon

An Olio Potreda    A Sirloyn of Beef Royal

Minc'd Pyes    Orange Pudding

Larks Ragoust    Legg of Lamb forc'd    Cutlets of Pork Grill'd

A Beef Pye in Blood    Hogs feet & Ears    A Fricasy of Rabbets    A Pottage La Reine of Patridges

Chicken a La forc'e

A Sallad    Sweet Breads Larded rost    Sheeps Tongu's    Fine Puddings of Sorts    Petit Patyes    Slices of Veal    A Sallad

Cardoons    Eggs La Switz

A Powdoe

A Bisque of Pidgeons    Pidgeons Compoté    Fryd Brawn    A Haunch of Venison rost forc'd & Larded

A Tort de Moyle    Oyster Loaves    A Bacon Tort    Minc'd Pyes

A Flesh Pudding    Turkeys a La Dobe    A Fillo of Pullets with a Temperade of thickens

Andoo-lies

To Change    To Change

A Smoak'd Goose & Cabbage    A Chine of Mutton & Collops

A Twenty five Dish Table.

From *The Complete Practical Cook* (1730) by Charles Carter.

40

# The Second Courfe.

Four Plates to Change.
Aspara gus.
Moreles and Troufles.
Sham-pinions Ragoust.
Cray Fish butter'd.
Where the King sat.

A Sallad Mogundy
Pheasants 3 Partridges 8 half larded
Lobsters & Crabs Pyled
Tongues Sli-ced
A Cream Tart.
Puff of Curd.
A white Pot.
Sker-rets butter'd
Cocks 6. Plovers 6. Snipes 12
A Tansey.
A Pippin Jelly Tart.
Squob Pidgeons 24.
Fri-nage de Tour
Car-doones
Oyster stued
Potargoe.
Quails 28.
Rago sweet bread
Pickles of sorts
Pota toe but
Larks rost 36.
Cavear.
Arti-choke
A Patty of Spanish Potatoes &c.
A Prunella Tart
A Tansey
Curlews 6 Redshanks 8.
Fry'd Cream.
Potted Venison
Fritters French
A Lamprey Pye
Lamb rostin Joynts
Sturgeon & Salmon Sowc'd
Ducks 4 Teals 8.
A Herring Sallad

From *The Complete Practical Cook* (1730) by Charles Carter.

41

A light supper (of leftovers) might be provided in the evening and the day would end with tea or chocolate, served wherever convenient.

Although there was plenty of choice in wealthy households like Ham, polite guests were only supposed to eat what they were offered. So unless their appetite was hearty and the service assiduous, they would not necessarily taste every dish on the table. When they wanted a drink they had to summon a servant who brought them a glass of wine or beer and then took it away to refill and give to somebody else. The wine was kept in a 'cistern' or wine cooler full of cold water which stood on the floor. (There is a marble cistern in the marble dining-room, as well as a copper one in the buttery.)

Polite guests were also supposed to accept any special dishes or drinks that their hosts offered them. This offered scope for some nasty practical jokes, as the Duke of Lauderdale discovered to his cost when intruding on one of Charles II's intimate dinner parties. The King, wanting to teach Lauderdale a lesson, offered him a glass of syllabub. Normally this was a delicious drink made by adding wine or cider to cream or milk, along with sugar and other flavourings, but on this occasion it consisted of something different . . .

According to Thomas, Earl of Ailesbury, Charles II, after drinking heavily, asked the master of the house for a double glass of syllabub to refresh him. By prearranged signal, the king knew which side to drink from before offering Lauderdale the other half, which contained horse urine! The unsuspecting duke duly drank it, and politely swore that no person had such a taste as his majesty! The urine soon had the desired effect; Lauderdale became so sick that he had to be carried out. The Earl of Ailesbury comments that Charles II was never troubled again by this unwanted guest.

'The Prospect of the inside of St George's Hall, with the King and Knights dining'.

Wenceslaus Hollar (1607–1677), print, 1672.

# LATER domestic life *at* HAM HOUSE

OUTSIDE the seventeenth-century kitchen and larder there is a display of later domestic equipment, including a 'hastener' of c. 1820 (a tin-lined backless cupboard used for warming a dinner service in front of the kitchen fire), a Victorian fire extinguisher and coal waggon, both on wheels, and Edwardian servants' bells.

The National Trust Shop is in the room used as the servants' hall in Victorian times.

Also in the basement (but not open to the public) is a Victorian wine cellar fitted with handsome iron racks, a Victorian cold store room, and a scullery with an eighteenth-century stone sink.

Outside the house there is a charming dairy, with tiled walls and marble slabs supported on delicate cows' legs, and an early nineteenth-century ice-house (which was converted into an air raid shelter during the Second World War). These can be seen by appointment.

The cook, wearing the tools of his trade.
Martin Engelbrecht (1684–1756), German/French print, c. 1720.

'A Tale of the tubbs or Rome's masterpiece defeated', a satirical print dated 1679 containing pictures of TUBS and a pair of WEIGHING SCALES.

Note the GAME RACK on a pulley and large number of BASKETS and COOPERED VESSELS used for transporting and storing food in this Dutch kitchen.

Print after a painting by David Teniers (1610–1690).

# *Further* READING

SEVENTEENTH–CENTURY COOKERY BOOKS WHICH ARE EASY TO GET HOLD OF:

*The Court and Kitchen of Elizabeth Cromwell*, first published in 1664, reprinted by Cambridgeshire Libraries, Publications Committee, c/o Central Library, Broadway, Peterborough, 1983, with glossary and notes by Mary Liquorice.

*The Compleat Cook* and *A Queen's Delight*, first published in 1655 as two of a trilogy entitled *The Queens Closet Opened* by W. M. The 1671 editions of these two books, which deal with cookery, were reprinted in facsimile by Prospect Books, 45 Lamont Rd, London SW10 OHU, in 1983.

*The Closet of the Eminently Learned Sir Kenelme Digbie Kt Opened*, first published in 1669 and reprinted by Philip Lee Warner, London, in 1910, with introduction, notes and glossary by Anne Macdonell.

John Evelyn – *Acetaria. A Discourse of Sallets*, first published in 1699, reprinted in facsimile by Prospect Books, 45 Lamont Rd, London SW10 OHU, in 1982.

Ann Blencowe – *The Receipt Book of Ann Blencowe A.D. 1694*, reprinted by Adelphi, London, in 1925 with an introduction by George Saintsbury.


GENERAL BACKGROUND

Caroline Davidson – *A Woman's Work is Never Done: A History of Housework in the British Isles, 1650–1950*, Chatto and Windus, London, 1982.

Caroline Davidson – 'The restoration of the kitchen at Ham House' in *Petits Propos Culinaires, a journal containing essays and notes on food, cookery and cookery books*, published by Prospect Books (see above), issues 12 (Nov 1982) and 15 (Nov 1983).

Caroline Davidson – 'The Seventeenth-Century Kitchen at Ham House' in *The V & A Album 2*, Templegate Publishing with the Associates of the V & A, 1983.

Barbara Ketcham Wheaton – *Savouring the Past. The French Kitchen and Table from 1300 to 1789*, Chatto and Windus, London, 1983.

Louise Conway Belden — *The Festive Tradition. Table Decoration and Desserts in America, 1650–1900*, W. W. Norton & Company, New York and London, 1983.

# The ASSOCIATES *of the* VICTORIA and ALBERT MUSEUM

The following companies and individuals take a particular interest in the Museum and channel their support through the Museum's charity, The Associates of the V&A:

ASSOCIATES
Arthur Andersen & Co
The Baring Foundation
Bonas and Company
Christie's
Colnaghi & Co
Commercial Union Assurance Company
Charles Letts (Holdings) Limited
Mobil
Oppenheimer Charitable Trust

Rose & Hubble Limited
J. Sainsbury plc
Sotheby's
John Swire & Sons Limited
Thames Television

INDIVIDUAL BENEFACTORS AND ASSOCIATES
The Sirdar and Begum Aly Aziz
Sir Duncan Oppenheim
Mrs Basil Samuel

SPONSORS Through The Associates of the V&A, the following companies, organisations and individuals have sponsored Galleries, Exhibitions, Scholarships, Lectures, Concerts and Catalogues at the V&A since 1981:

The Countess Ahlefeldt
The Aquarius Trust
B.A.D.A.
G. P. & J. Baker Limited
Bankers Trust Company
The Baring Foundation
Cariplo Bank
The Countryside Commission
The Daily Telegraph
Express Newspapers plc
H. J. Heinz Charitable Trust

Ilford Limited
Jaeger
Sirge Lifar
The Linbury Trust
The Merrill Trust
Mobil
Pearson plc
Pirelli
Mrs Basil Samuel
Trusthouse Forte
United Technologies

# The FRIENDS *of the* VICTORIA and ALBERT MUSEUM

Existing within the framework of The Associates, the following Corporate Friends give their support to the Museum:

CORPORATE FRIENDS

Alan Hutchinson Publishing Company Limited
Albert Amor Limited
Antiques Porcelain Company
Artists Cards Limited
Ashtead Decorative & Fine Arts Society
Asprey & Company
Bank of England Arts Society
Bankers Trust Company
Blairman & Sons Limited
British Petroleum
Chase Manhattan Bank
Cobra & Bellamy
Coutts & Co Bankers
Crabtree & Evelyn Limited
Cyril Humphris
Donohoe
Goldsmiths' Company
Hotspur Limited
John Keil Limited
Kennedy Brookes plc
Ian Logan Limited

London & Provincial Antique Dealers' Association
Madame Tussaud's Limited
Marks & Spencer plc
The Medici Society Limited
Mendip Decorative and Fine Arts Society
Barbara Minto Limited
W. H. Patterson Fine Arts Limited
Pearson plc
Charles Pfister Inc.
Phillips Auctioneers
S. J. Phillips plc
Phillips Petroleum
Pickering & Chatto
R T Z Services Limited
South Molton Antiques Limited
Spink & Son Limited
Stair & Co
The Fine Art Society Limited
The Wellcome Foundation Limited
William Bedford Antiques
Winifred Williams
World of Islam Festival Trust

INDIVIDUAL FRIENDS support the Museum both financially and by giving voluntary help, thus forming a personal link with the V&A.